Season of
Devotion

A Gift for you

To: _____

From: _____

Season of
Devotion

By

Steven Jacobs

Table of Contents

Introduction   1

1. A Painting Of Holiness   3
2. Following The Trail   5
3. Looking Through The Wrong End   7
4. Where's Your Confidence?   9
5. Where He Leads I Will Follow   11
6. Practice Makes Perfect   13
7. Soaring Like An Eagle   15
8. Alone And Vulnerable   17
9. Heroes   19
10. Lip Smacking Good   21
11. Balancing Act   23
12. The Hunt   25
13. Eliminating Scents   27
14. Camaraderie   29
15. Are You Blending In?   31
16. Commitment   33
17. Decoy Deception   35
18. Dog With A Purpose   37
19. Fair Weather Hunter   39
20. It's A Family Affair   41
21. Paralyzed With Fear   43
22. One Slug Please   45
23. Thinking Out Of The Box   47

24. A Gentle Patience   49

25. Giving And Receiving   51

26. Armchair Hunter   53

27. The Trophy Feast   55

28. Sizing Up The Hunt   57

29. Oh, Taste And See   59

30. Focused And Tuned In   61

31. Quick Draw   65

32. The Great Awaited Day   67

33. Shoot It, Then Eat It   69

34. Experiencing The Whole Package   71

35. No Waiting Required   73

36. Keep Your Eyes On The Light   75

37. Success Can Have Regrets   77

38. A Sweet Savor   79

39. Ready - Aim - Fire   81

40. Altitude Revelations   83

41. Tethered In The Stand   85

42. Devoted To The Chase   87

43. God's Creation   89

44. Anticipation   91

45. Prepare Or Despair   93

SEASON OF DEVOTION

Devotional for the Hunter

Introduction

A great white hunter I do not claim to be, but I do enjoy participating in the sport, and reading of other hunters experiences. As I get older, I begin to see things a little differently than I did as a teen hunter. Recently, a medical condition has greatly changed my outlook on life and hunting practices. I will be referring to my hunting buddy, Gary, occasionally in the pages to follow. He has helped me in the field because of my condition and has inspired some of the thoughts written herein. As I looked at different aspects of hunting, many applications concerning the Christian walk began to surface. There are a few fishing parallels thrown in, but, I am not the character of Hemingway's The Old Man and the Sea. I will share what God has laid upon my heart. It is my desire that you will be challenged to have a closer walk with our Heavenly Father. His desire is for His children to love and obey Him; but quite often, we get sidetracked with other things and lose sight of what is most important. We are to love God, love others, and connect the former with the latter. Put on your hunting clothes, pour a cup of coffee, and join me as we enjoy Gods creation together and seek to find a deeper love for Him.

A Painting Of Holiness

Some of the closest times I have felt with the Lord is when I am in a boat, hunting, or simply enjoying being outdoors. Summer of 2008 held one of those awe-inspiring moments. Four of us were on Kodiak Island making our way in a boat up the remaining ten miles of a forty mile long bay. As we were delighting in the sights and smells of this wilderness, we were all lost in our own thoughts. Now, I would like to paint a picture of what I experienced.

Several thousand feet above us, the mountain had a headdress of snow with intermingled meadows of green grass and shrubs. The slope was steep and plummeted down to intersect the blue-green water and continued to the mountain's foundation a hundred feet below the water surface. Interspersed in the varying surfaces of the mountains were silver ribbons of cascading water coming from the snow fields above, hurdling headlong to the placid bay below. High above the junction of land and water, I could see eagles soaring on the thermals. Looking across the surface of the water, salmon were jumping on their desperate journey to the river of our destination. Their life would end either as a result of spawning or as protein for the many Kodiak bears. From the bears ambling along on the beach to the mountain goats high up in the grass meadows, all of creation seemed to be in a feeding frenzy during the short time of summer on the island. The concentration of bears increased as we neared the end of the bay. They were either eating grass or trying to catch salmon using various techniques, some of which were quite entertaining. The teddy bear syndrome set in as I watched them play and interact with each other and

3

with an opportunistic fox. Reality would set in when a fight over food suddenly erupted, ending the silence with growls and roars. I was totally captivated by this buffet of sights, and sounds. The phrase "Holy, Holy, Thou art Holy" kept going through my mind. God had created this outdoor cathedral for me to see and experience at this time. Truly He is the Creator and Sustainer of all.

"Give unto the LORD the glory due unto his name; worship the LORD in the beauty of holiness." Psalm 29:2

Verse: Revelation 4:8; Psalm 139:1-18; Psalm 29:2-9

Following The Trail

Over the years, Gary and I have tracked several deer. The scenario would go something like this. I would come in from hunting after dark to a phone message of "I hit a deer, could you come up?" I would grab boots and lantern and take off. The two of us would go to the site of the shot where the bloodhound in us would kick in and off we would go. One night his wife, Shelley, came with us as it was her deer we were tracking. We were out in the swamp trying to unravel the blood trail. The swamp was wet and thick with brush and swamp grass. There was a stream running through it. He and I crossed the stream and were totally absorbed in following the trail when we heard a faint voice behind us. It was Shelley in a pitifully, forlorn voice saying, "I guess it is every person for themselves." We had left her on the opposite side of the stream with no light and no aid from either of us. After a laugh at her expense, we tried to keep better tabs on her for the rest of the evening.

Application: Today there are a lot of Christians with the Lone Ranger philosophy. It is every person for themselves going through the adventures of life. The struggling brethren can be overlooked and ignored because we are too busy with our own life. The need for discipleship and mentoring is being grossly disregarded, and a price is being paid in an immature, needy Christian society. Looking at scriptural examples, we see that Paul included many people in his ministry. Jesus mentored twelve men that set the world on fire. Was it easy? No. He is our example, and we are to do likewise. God desires for a partnership of believers, no Lone Rangers.

"These things speak, and exhort, and rebuke with all authority. Let no man despise thee." Titus 2:15

Verse: Titus 2 (chapter)

Looking Through The Wrong End

Most hunters own a pair of binoculars. The obvious use for them is to visually bring distant items up close for better observation. When our children were younger, and now the grandchildren, they liked to look into the binoculars through the wrong end which shrinks the objects to look small and very distant. They would be completely entertained with this visual inconsistency.

Application: Sometimes we try to minimize God so that our small minds can understand Him better. When we read of Biblical encounters with God, the person had a fear of losing his life because of it. Yet, we attempt to bring this awe-inspiring God to our level and treat Him as a good buddy. He has been brought down to our level so that we can better relate to Him. I like what Isaiah writes as a result of his vision of God. God was sitting on His throne high and lifted up shrouded in all His glory. The view of God we see through Isaiah's eyes of the mighty Creator and Sustainer, was so great, that Isaiah thought he was going to die from the experience. What is our view of God? Is He high and lifted up or have we taken Him off of His throne and brought down to our level? If He is truly high and lifted up, then our outlook of praise and worship will reflect that. We will more readily leave our burdens and cares at His feet and let Him deal with them. Where is God in your life? If we look through the magnification end of the binoculars at God, and learn what the Scripture is teaching us of Him, we will see that the same God Isaiah saw is by our side and wants to be a part of our life. He is not the distant figure as seen through the wrong end of the binoculars. How big is your God? If need be, put

Him back on the throne.

"In the year that king Uzziah died I saw also the Lord sitting upon a throne, high and lifted up, and his train filled the temple." Isaiah 6:1

Verse: Isaiah 6:1-13

Where is Your Confidence?

Years ago, a friend from church called me and asked for my help. As the story began to unfold, he had been duck hunting on a rivers backwater. The water there was at least six feet deep with approximately three feet of silt on the bottom. He was alone in this watery haven when somehow his canoe tipped over, and he went overboard with all his gear. His waders filled up, and the situation became a battle for his life. He struggled to keep his head above water to avoid drowning. Perilously close to death, the slight current and his flailing arms had taken him close enough to shore that he was able to get out. At the outset he had confidence that his waders were going to give him comfort and keep him dry, but they nearly cost him his life. All this took place not a quarter mile from a busy highway where commuters were totally unaware that a man was in a battle for his life. His subsequent phone call was a request for me to use my scuba gear and attempt retrieval of his brand new shot gun. It was a lost cause because of the depth of silt on the bottom.

Application: The world puts confidence in a myriad of things to insure that they get to Heaven. It may be that they are a good person or that they go to church regularly. It may be something they do or do not observe. Whatever it is, they hope to escape the fires of hell. The very thing they put their confidence in will be what will cost them an eternity with Christ. There is only one way to Heaven and that is through the work of Jesus Christ on the cross. We need to believe what He has done. No work on our part or by anyone else will get us to Heaven. Jesus said that "I am the way, the truth, and the life; no man cometh unto the

Father but by Me." He did not say He was one of many ways, but He is the only way to Heaven.

Christians can be like those who were driving by without a clue of the struggle going on. Ask yourself, do I have a heart for the lost and dying world or am I comfortable with where I am and have no real desire to be in the rescue business?

"For all have sinned, and come short of the glory of God;" Romans 3:23

Verse: John 14:1-6; Romans 3:23; Ephesians 2:1-10; John 3:16-21

Where He Leads I Will Follow

Shortly after coming in from the woods one night there was a telephone call from a new neighbor next door to us. The caller told me that he had shot a deer and it ran onto our property. He was seeking permission to pursue it. It was fine with me, but not knowing him I wanted to accompany him. He took me to the spot where he had taken the shot and proceeded to follow the track. There was a light skiff of snow on the ground that made tracks and blood droplets obvious. He was new to hunting and, so far, had really enjoyed the sport. Letting him lead, we went about thirty feet when I stopped him. He was doing a great job of tracking except for the fact that he was going backwards. When I pointed this out to him he did not believe me. After a short lesson and close examination of the track, he decided to give my way a try. A short time later, we were dragging the deer out of the swamp.

Application: In II Timothy we read that we are to accurately interpret the Word of God. As we study it, we are to interpret it in light of the context and other Scripture. Problems arise when we make it say what we want. God tells us in Deuteronomy that we are not to add or take away from His Word. This carries true all the way through the book of Revelation. The misreading of Scripture can affect the individual in varying degrees from minor misinterpretation, which will hinder his walk with the Lord, to the extent that it will take the person in the opposite direction of salvation itself. Let us be cautious in our interpretation of the written Word of God so as not to lead others or ourselves in the wrong direction.

"Study to show thyself approved unto God, a workman that needeth not to be ashamed, rightly dividing the word of truth." II Timothy 2:15

Verse: Deuteronomy 4:1-2; II Timothy 2:14-16

Practice Makes Perfect

The season is getting closer, and if you are like most hunters, the gun or bow come out, and we begin to practice shooting at targets. Every year we think that we will shoot throughout the year to hone our abilities; but most of the time, we get too busy and the seasons roll around, and we realize another year has slipped by without putting a single shot into the target. As we practice, our shots become consistent, and we are confident that we can get the job done. Hopefully, the practice pays off with meat in the freezer. What about the times when you flat out miss? We want to blame the equipment, weather, or whatever else; but the truth of the matter is that it was hunter error. It is the missed or poorly placed shots that tend to haunt us. Quite often, it is a trophy animal or a sure shot that is missed. Overconfidence can be a big factor at times.

Application: In Bible college, I was taught that a simple definition for sin is missing the mark. "What mark?" You may ask. Our target is obedience to God, following in His footsteps, and living in accordance to His will. The more we practice in His strength, the better we will get in obeying His standards.

Target practice is a lifelong discipline, and there will be times when we will miss. We will want to blame anyone or anything for the sin in our life, but the truth of the matter is that the blame and responsibility rest entirely upon our own shoulders. I John 1:9 tells us, when we ask for forgiveness, He will forgive and our fellowship and communication with Him will be restored. What about times when we miss the target and it lingers in our minds as a point of failure?

The beauty of it is that God has removed this sin from us as far as the east is from the west. We need to stop dwelling on it and move on with Christ. So as we practice and get more precise with our weapon, we should think of the fact that the more we walk in obedience with God we will become more familiar with Him and His desires for our life. We need to constantly call upon His strength and wisdom to keep us on the target. There needs to be a total dependency upon God and not on ourselves. A final thought comes to mind, when we miss the trophy animal and we experience the sinking feeling, ask the question, "Do I have a similar sinking feeling when I disobey my Lord and Savior?"

"I press toward the mark for the prize of the high calling of God in Christ Jesus." Philippians 3:14

Verse: Philippians 3 (chapter)

Soaring Like An Eagle

The hunt was over, and with mixed emotions, we were due to fly out of the Alaskan wilderness and head for home. Getting back to our families was cause for excitement, but leaving the sights and smells of this untamed land was definitely leaving an empty feeling in the pit of our stomachs. The plane touched down on the mountain top airstrip where the guide had thrown the rocks off to the side and had attempted to level the hummocks that are indicative of tundra. The bush plane taxied up to the pile of meat, gear, and antlers that we had piled alongside the airstrip. It had been a successful hunt with two caribou, a moose, and a wolf to the credit of three hunters. After the pilot asked the weight of two of us, he began to pick up meat and gear, estimating their weight and keeping a mental tally as he loaded. He wanted as much of the meat and gear as possible to go on the first flight, so the next load would be one hunter and the antlers. When he reached the golden weight, that only he knew, of getting on all he could load and still be able to fly, he informed us that the plane was overweight; but by using the air currents he thought we could lift off. Now, I am not a pilot, but these words did not endow me with a warm fuzzy feeling. Two of us were about to put our lives in the hands of this tall red bearded bush pilot and reluctantly climbed in. You could feel the rough surface through the balloon tires as we went down the strip, trying to gain speed. Would the landing gear even hold together until lift off? The words of the pilot, "I think we can get off," were echoing in my head as the strip was fast disappearing. We used up the whole length of the strip and were then out of mountain.

The plane shot into space; but instead of soaring to the heavens like an eagle, we sank into the valley flapping like an overweight turkey. I think the angels called in the reserves as they managed to slowly pull the plane out of the sink and caused it to climb. We slowly climbed out of the valley skimming over the next mountain, and we were now on our way back to civilization.

Application: God wants us to shed our burdens and soar with Him. Often times, we do not want to leave our excess baggage along the side of the airstrip; but instead, we insist on bringing it along. Our excess can be past hurts, sins that God has forgiven us for, but we cannot forgive ourselves, legalism, or anything else that hinders our walk with Him. We drag along the baggage so that instead of soaring like a graceful eagle floating on the thermals, we are flapping around like a fat turkey that can hardly clear the trees. Shall we leave behind the excess baggage and soar with Him?

"Cast thy burden upon the LORD, and he shall sustain thee: he shall never suffer the righteous to be moved."
Psalm 55:22

Verse: Isaiah 40:27-31; Psalm 55:22; Matthew 11:28-30

16

Alone And Vulnerable

Throughout our hunting careers, we have probably all experienced a time when the hair on the back of our necks stood on end, and a cold chill went over us like fog over a marsh. Sometimes it was a sound or just our imaginations that ran away with us. My daughter experienced such feelings this last deer season. Just before dark, a doe had come out to the edge of the field when she shot it. The deer ran off into some trees, and after a little time elapsed, my daughter went after it. They did a cat and mouse thing; the deer keeping just ahead of her with a row of pine trees between them. The evening light was now completely gone and it was pitch dark. She called me on her cell phone, and I left right away to help her. She had given me a familiar landmark and waited for me there. Upon my arrival, I turned off the engine and noticed that there were several coyotes yapping very close to her. Later, I was to find out that as she stood there they had been coming closer and closer to her location. She had no light except what came from her cell phone pad. Having not seen a tree suitable to climb, she started to sing and talk to herself to ward off the hordes of beasts. We retrieved the deer and left the coyotes without even a scrap to eat.

Application: There are times in our walk with the Lord when the valleys are deep, dark, and frightening. Circumstances seem to overwhelm us, and we are faced with fear and uncertainty. We feel alone and vulnerable, yet we need to draw on the promises that God is by our side and will not forsake us.

"Be strong and of a good courage, fear not, nor be afraid of them: for the LORD thy God, he it is that doth go with thee; he will not fail thee, nor forsake thee." Deuteronomy 31:6

Verse: Psalm 37:28; Psalm 23:4-6

Heroes

There are organizations that are making inroads into changing the sport of hunting as we know it today. Some hunters are quite passionate in taking up positions to block any possible changes in these areas. Many questions and theories arise when one observes these battles. As sportsmen we may get fired up over such debates, but do we respond in like manner when our religious freedoms and morals are being attacked? I am afraid that if it came right down to it, we would not stand as firm for our religious rights as others. There are and have been many brothers and sisters around the world faced with this and have paid with their lives or, beatings and imprisonment. Changing the quote from Patrick Henry, could we say "Give me GOD or give me death"? In Hebrews, we see a brief list of faithful heroes who rose to the challenge and paid the price. As we read through this passage, may it give us strength and encouragement that if, or when, the time comes we too might stand faithful for God's morals and for the religious freedoms that we now enjoy. Let it also serve as a reminder to pray for those around the world who are faced with religious persecution on a daily basis.

"But without faith it is impossible to please him: for he that cometh to God must believe that he is, and that he is a rewarder of them that diligently seek him." Hebrews 11:6

Verse: Hebrews 11:1-40

Lip Smacking Good

There are many forms of baiting used throughout the hunting world. Where legal, there may be anything from corn, carrots, sugar beets, donuts and yogurt to animal carcasses. Some would be quite appealing, like the load of bakery goods I used one year for bear. Other baits are nothing short of disgusting. Regardless of what we think, the many varied irresistible baits are lip smacking good for the intended game. The idea is that we are appealing to one of the basic needs of the animal and are trying to lure it in so that we can make a shot. If all goes well, the shot is made. The trophy is recovered, and the hunt is over.

Application: I believe this is a picture of what Satan does to Christians. He knows exactly what the weak point is for each person. He uses that knowledge to lay out a bait, or temptation, that we will have a hard time refusing. The sole purpose is that we will not be able to refuse the temptation and will succumb to the sin, rendering us useless for Christ. We see that Paul was concerned with the possibility that he would give in to temptation and be ineffective for Christ. We too should be on a constant vigil against this in our life.

We also see that Satan is referred to as a roaring lion, seeking whom he may devour. Ladies and gentlemen, this is serious business, and there is no room for lazy Christians. We need to be ever aware of the wiles of Satan and resist him at all cost. The result will be that he will flee from us. We can live a victorious life thanks to Christ and the work He has done.

"Submit yourselves therefore to God. Resist the devil, and he will flee from you.

Draw nigh to God, and he will draw nigh to you. Cleanse your hands, ye sinners; and purify your hearts, ye double minded." James 4:7, 8

Verse: I Corinthians 9:26, 27; I Peter 5:6-11

Balancing Act

Balance plays an important role in the outdoor activities that we enjoy. For example, balance in a canoe or on a boat is crucial unless there is a desire to get wet. Balance during hunting or hiking activities is desired so as not to fall and sustain injury or to fall off elevated surfaces. The medical problem I have has rendered my equilibrium almost useless. Hence, after falling on numerous occasions with a loaded gun, I have altered my hunting tactics. With no balance, the rolling swells of Lake Michigan have made for some interesting moments almost resulting in an unexpected swim. Even with good balance, I think that most people have experienced moments when they are walking along, and suddenly look up at the world from a different perspective and are wondering how they got there.

Application: Most of us can relate our life to a balancing act and that there are times when we do not fare too well. How do we hit the proper balance of job and family? Our careers are the source of meeting our needs with financial means; but the family is a gift from God, and He expects us to raise our children in such a way that is pleasing to Him. Do we date our mate or are we so caught up in our careers that they become a stranger to us? We struggle with the proper balance of vacation time versus work schedule. We struggle with church and ministry time versus family time. What about the subject of improper balance of our hunt time versus other responsibilities during hunting season? God has a desire for us to lead a balanced life and not one of extremes. Are we willing to ask Him to balance our life in such a way that there are no missed opportunities in whatever He wants to accomplish through us?

"To every thing there is a season, and a time to every purpose under the heaven:" Ecclesiastes 3:1

Verse: Ecclesiastes 3:1-9; Ephesians 5:15-16

The Hunt

I have always had a dream of hunting dangerous game. The idea of going after an animal that can rearrange your anatomy in a blink of an eye is tantalizing to me. To my great enjoyment, I have watched bears during a hunt in Alaska and had the pleasure of hiking on Kodiak Island to view the huge Kodiak bears, also the experience of hunting black bear in the Upper Peninsula of Michigan. One hunt was in the transitional land between high ground and a vast swamp. The evergreen trees were thick and the floor was spongy because the water table was just under the surface. The oppressing silence felt like a heavy blanket weighing me down. The only sound heard was the raspy call of an occasional crow as it flew over. My blind consisted of a wooden two by four enclosure which was wrapped with a layer of wide sand paper from a huge industrial roll. The roof was inches from my head as I sat in a chair looking out a small slit in the front wall. Even though it was mid afternoon, the woods were dimly lit. Sunlight did not penetrate very deep through the thick canopy. I was enjoying the solitude of the afternoon when I began to notice a faint sound. Straining to identify what and where the sound was emanating from I realized that it was unlike anything I had heard before. In fact, it sounded like the soft footfall of what I expected a bear to make as it walked. Ever so slowly the sound came closer, first from behind, then right beside my blind. I began to wonder if I was to be host to a furry, four legged, man eating bruin in my flimsy blind. My finger was on the trigger, and my thumb was on the safety. Not having a port hole in the side of the blind, I waited for the bear to come into the peripheral of the slot in the front of the blind. I did not think of the possible dangers of having a bear just outside the blind, but focused on the possibility of being able to get a shot at it. The creature that was making the sound never materialized, but walked away and was absorbed into the ominous silence.

Application: I would like this entry to be a tribute to those men and women who are doing battle with the most savage and cunning predator of all. Man. With a son-in-law in the armed service and having been in combat, I began to take on a new appreciation for the sacrifices and dangers these men and women put themselves into on a daily basis to fight for our freedom and the freedom of others. Having grown up in the Vietnam era and seen the anti-war sentiment of the times, there was often little love lost on those who sacrificially served. Some of those sentiments are prevalent today with the Iraqi war. These warriors should receive our respect and gratitude for what they endure. May our prayers be felt by those who are serving and may we never let them think that we are ungrateful.

"To the praise of the glory of his grace, wherein he hath made us accepted in the beloved." Ephesians 1:16

Verse: Colossians 1:3

Eliminating Scents

One thing that the hunting marketing media has emphasized is the dire need to cover up odor. The caution taken for wind direction, and what is touched or rubbed against is now becoming archaic. There is scent covering soap to wash the body with and odor free laundry detergent that has the ability to clean and wash away all human scent. A spray can be used over all your body to eliminate any little scent gremlin that did not get zapped already. There is scent block clothing and scent block blinds. The latest to the market now is scent block gum so that the animals cannot smell your breath. Members of the animal kingdom tend to find the smell of man very offensive and will avoid its source at all cost.

Application: This makes me think of our lives as Christians. At salvation, we were washed clean with the blood of Christ, but then what? Sometimes we feel that once we were washed that is it. According to I John, we need a continual washing to maintain proper fellowship with God. When sin is in our life we do not need to be re-cleansed in terms of our salvation, but there is a need to be cleansed for the communication between God and us to be restored. That is why when Jesus washed the feet of the disciples and Peter wanted to be totally washed, Jesus told him it was not necessary. Peter had already been washed in salvation; but he needed the dirt of the world to be washed off, meaning his walk cleaned up. We, as hunters, take great care for our physical odors when it comes to hunting, but how much care do we take of our spiritual body odor?

"If we confess our sins, he is faithful and just to forgive us our sins, and to cleanse us from all unrighteousness."
I John 1:9

Verse: I John 1 (chapter)

Camaraderie

There are times when I go fishing or hunting alone, just me, the great outdoors, and my own thoughts. Then there are times when it is great fun and enjoyment for a group sharing the same interest to get together and enjoy the sport of hunting or fishing. Whether it is a large group or just two, the time is spent in getting to know each other more by sharing concerns and joys. There is usually light joking and laughing at ourselves and each other. Of course there is time spent in getting some shooting done or bringing in a fish or two. As a result of these types of activities, there are some friendships formed that may not have happened otherwise.

Application: Generally, men tend to face life's problems alone. The problem may be in the form of a temptation that is a real struggle. It may be a financial situation or a family burden. We tend to try to solve or get through them the best we can and often times, as a result, we become weary Christians. We get to the point where we cannot assess the situation logically or see it for what it really is. This is where those friendships are of great benefit.

When Amalek fought against Israel, all went well as long as Moses held his hands up. As they dropped, the battle would turn in favor of Amalek. Moses had two men hold up his hands until the battle was won. Sometimes that is what we need when we get weary in the battle. A friend needs to help hold up our hands. Friends are there for sounding boards and to help see the situation more clearly. This becomes more natural as friendships are cultivated. We need to ask ourselves if we are willing to help, or receive help, from another. True friendships will hold each other accountable through temptations and trials. We need to realize that we are vulnerable when we are weary and need to draw upon Christian friendships. Do we sharpen each other or do we tend to be of little help and dull the edge of each other?

"Iron sharpeneth iron; so a man sharpeneth the countenance of his friend." Proverbs 27:17

Verse: Exodus 17:8-16; Proverbs 27:17;
Proverbs 27:9

Are You Blending In?

The big money maker today is in clothing for the discriminate hunter. There is camouflage for every form of hunting that one is to do, from snow to swamps to woods to desert and everything in between. Recently, on a waterfowl hunt, the guys put on their camouflage and really looked good. If I were a duck, there would be little question in my mind that these guys were serious about disappearing from sight. As for me, my theory is to think blend in and hold a branch in front of my face. My gear consisted of desert camouflage coat and digital camouflage pants and shirt. Any duck flying over was sure to be impressed.

Let's start with Hunter Orange. Now, here is a real blend in situation. This is to let the hunter stand out for safety reasons during gun season. Along with the sale of this the marketers tell us that deer are color blind, so this "in your face" orange does not bother them. We now come to when the animal being hunted has a more refined taste for clothing. The hunter has to look exactly like the surroundings because of the close proximity with the animal. It is not enough to look like a tree, but now you need to look like the species of tree you are in and the color of the season. The idea is to blend in and imitate your surroundings to the point that the animal cannot identify your form nor can they detect any movement.

Application: As Christians, we are to stand out from our surroundings. We are to be a light in a darkened world and to be the salt of the earth. All too often we want to blend in and imitate the world and "enjoy" what it has to offer. God is asking us to come out and be separate; but we often want to look, talk, act, and live like the world, which is in direct contradiction to God. As we put on our camouflage to imitate our surroundings, let us think of how we are to imitate Christ in our actions and speech, and yet stand out from the world around us.

"Let your light so shine before men, that they may see your good works, and glorify your Father which is in heaven." Matthew 5:16

Verses: Ephesians 5:1-17; Matthew 5:13-16

Commitment

An interesting phenomenon often takes place during goose season. A flock of geese will come in and undergo fire from the hunters carefully concealed on the ground. A bird goes down and the flock will fly off. Momentarily, the mate to the shot goose will often circle back to see where its mate is. When this happens, the hunter may have a chance to shoot that goose also. The fact that a goose will often return to the place of danger to find its mate is cause for us to reflect on the commitment of the pair.

Application: Research has disproved that a goose will mate for life, but in fact mates for a season. The illustration falls short here because we are to be united with our spouse for life. But time and again we see where a relationship will come under fire, and a spouse will fly off with the flock and never look back. Are we committed to our marriages to the point that we will face all dangers and obstacles to the relationship together? Will we guard our relationship from all outside influences that can destroy our marriage? Guard your heart and value your marriage as a rare and valuable treasure.

"Let thy fountain be blessed: and rejoice with the wife of thy youth." Proverbs 5:18

Verse: Proverbs 5 (chapter)

Decoy Deception

Part of the gear used for duck or goose hunting is a good spread of decoys. These are placed strategically so that the birds flying over will see what they think to be a flock feeding and will come within gun range of the waiting hunters. Some decoys are so lifelike I am sure they have been mistaken by hunters for the real deal. Even though a good spread has been the demise of many a bird, it is not a sure thing that others will come in. During my last goose hunt there were times when the geese coming in would veer off at the last moment and fly off not giving the spread of decoys in the corn field another thought. There was something they saw, or did not see, that made them suspicious. These birds probably had already been shot at several times before causing them to be very cautious.

Application: How many times have we been deceived by Satan, or our own desires, into thinking that the grass is greener on the other side of the fence? How many times has the glitter of that new toy convinced us that if it were pursued we would experience real happiness? Many of us, to our shame, still fall for the hollow promise of fulfillment and contentment if only we were to succumb to those decoys placed before us. Just as the bird veered off and lived for another day, we need to be cautious and learn to recognize what the authentic is and what a decoy is. This can be accomplished by getting closer to God and becoming so familiar with Him that we will recognize the imitation and have no desire for it. We need to come to the realization that true contentment comes only from God.

"Not that I speak in respect of want: for I have learned, in whatsoever state I am, therewith to be content." Philippians 4:11

Verse: Job 15:31; Ephesians 5:1-14; I John 3:1-12; Philippians 4:10-14

Dog With A Purpose

Back in the late seventies, southwest Lower Michigan was hit with a couple of hard winters which aided in the destruction of the pheasant population. It has never rebounded to where it was before the snow and ice. Before that time, our farm was a great spot for hunting pheasant. I would go out to the marsh in the afternoon after school, or after work, to hunt. When the dog saw me coming out of the house with a gun, she knew exactly what was going to happen. On the way to the field, she would be beside herself with excitement, running down the lane like she was on a caffeine high. Once we got to the tall marsh grasses, she would instantly be all business. She would range out, usually just the right distance, and keep looking back to me for approval and to be sure I was still there. She would keep her nose either to the ground or lift her head to sniff the air. None of my dogs were trained professionally, but they seemed to pick up what they were to do in spite of my feeble attempt to train them. The greatest moments were when the dog would go on point and then retrieve the downed bird. Hunting with the dog was a delight as I watched her respond to the clues she found. She would work her heart out for the pure enjoyment of it and to please me. Her eagerness and perseverance was truly inspirational.

Application: As I think of how my dogs would hunt, I am reminded of how the people of Berea (found in the book of Acts) diligently, and with great eagerness, examined the scriptures daily to see what truth was. They were comparing what they heard, with the written Word; to be sure that what they were being taught was true. This searching and daily digging into the Bible will cause growth and stability in the believers' life. We are exhorted to study for ourselves, learn of the truth written, and to become better acquainted with our heavenly Father. As the dog would follow the scent trail of the bird and works it out with tenacity, so are we to get into the Word and search for the treasures that are to be found. Are we passionate to learn more of the Godhead? Are we searching for ourselves or just lazily sitting back and receiving the findings of others?

"These were more noble than those in Thessalonica, in that they received the word with all readiness of mind, and searched the scriptures daily, whether those things were so." Acts 17:11

Verse: Acts 17:10-15; II Timothy 2:14-16; Ephesians 4:14-16

Fair Weather Hunter

Over time, I have found I have become a fair weather hunter. The days of going out, regardless of the weather, are slipping into the past. Now, I do not like to get cold, wet, hot, or bit by bugs. Looking at that list you may ask, then when do you go out? Well, sometimes I go out regardless, but other times I choose to throw another block of wood into the wood stove and grab a book or do something on the honey-do list. Knowing that these adverse conditions may present the best hunting opportunity still lacks incentive to get me out.

Application: If we look at our spiritual lives, we find often times we are fair weather Christians. When things are going well, we are praising the Lord and think that life is good. We are thankful for what the Lord is doing in our lives and are expressing our joy to others. But, when life gets a little rough, and a storm blows through, we often lose sight of the fact that God is also working to do His good pleasure in our lives. The fact that He uses adversity to strengthen us and to promote spiritual growth goes right out the window after the second blizzard. We begin to complain and question why He would do such a thing to me and lose all joy in our lives. Praise God that He is always in control and never is caught sleeping on the job. Everything coming into our lives has first passed over the desk of God, and He has stamped His seal of approval on it. This fact should make each one of us take courage in the midst of the storms of life and give thanks to Him. Can we be all-weather Christians, praising and thanking Him in the bad times as well as the good times? Remember just as in hunting, it is the bad weather that often results in the greatest trophy; so it is in our life. It is the rough times that produce the most growth and knowledge of our Savior.

"My brethren, count it all joy when ye fall into divers temptations; Knowing this, that the trying of your faith worketh patience." James 1:2, 3

Verse: James 1 (chapter)

It's A Family Affair

We have taken great joy in watching our children develop a love for the great out doors. They love hiking, hunting, fishing, and simply being outside. Conservation has become more of an interest to them as they realize the value of seasons and limits. Habitat became more of an issue to them once they began to hunt and saw first hand how it relates to wildlife. Having these values in common draws us together, especially during hunting season and in the summer when we can fish in the pond. It has created memories that I would not trade for anything. I have read time and time again that the future of hunting depends upon us as we instill the values upon our children and those we have influence over. If you do not have a son or daughter, then maybe you can take on the task of mentoring a child, imparting your knowledge and love for the outdoors to them.

Application: God has given us, as parents, a great responsibility and privilege to raise our children. Let us remember to teach God's morals and scriptural truths during the times when we get out and enjoy nature, whether hunting, fishing or hiking down a trail. Instead of making the outdoors a getaway by ourselves, why not consider including our children? God has created all things above, below, and on earth for the utilization and pleasure of man.

"In his hand are the deep places of the earth: the strength of the hills is his also." Psalm 95:4

Verse: Genesis 1; Psalm 95:1-5

Paralyzed with Fear

This entry is not related to hunting, but definitely has the flavor that many hunters may have experienced in the outdoors.

Years ago, I was in a missionary training program that prepared one to go to primitive tribes in remote places of the world to preach the Gospel of Christ. Part of the training consisted of a three day, two night hike along the Georgian Bay in Ontario, Canada. We were practicing compass travel, where we took turns leading the group of men off the trail, into the woods, and return to the trail once again. It was my turn to lead, and I can remember going through a beautiful semi-open wooded area. The ground was covered with lush green foliage that was over a foot tall. The group of about fifteen men trailed off behind me as we walked through this pristine area. Suddenly, I heard a buzzing sound. I had never heard a rattlesnake before, but I instantly knew that the sound I was hearing was the buzz of the rattles of such a snake. We had talked of the danger of these snakes on the trail we were hiking, and the measures to be taken if one were indeed encountered. I froze in my tracks as the staff leaders came closer. We could not locate the snake under the foliage, but it was obvious from the sound it was close by and not happy with me. The leaders told me to slowly back away from it. All I could picture was this viper hurling itself through the air and sinking it's fangs into my leg. I found I was literally paralyzed with fear. I could not force my feet to move from that spot; meanwhile, the viper was buzzing and the others in the group were trying to locate it. Finally, after much persuasion, I was able to back off and avoid a strike.

The snake was located, and now its rattles are in my desk as a reminder of my first encounter with a Mississauga Rattlesnake.

Application: There are times in the Christian life when we are paralyzed with fear. God may be asking a person to step out in faith and do something for Him. You need to evaluate for yourself what that task may be. It may be to teach a class, speak of Him to a friend, or to use a gift He has given you to strengthen the body of Christ. Fear has your feet rooted in a comfort zone even though God is encouraging you to take a step out. To take the step is to obey God's prompting and receive a blessing. To stay put and refuse to obey will bring stagnation and a loss of blessing to you and the ones you were to minister to. Can we rest upon the power of God and take that step?

"For God hath not given us the spirit of fear; but of power, and of love, and of a sound mind." II Timothy 1:7

Verse: II Timothy 1:6-14; Psalm 118:6; Proverbs 29:25

One Slug Please

My first year of deer hunting must have been around 1969. I was the proud owner of a 12 gauge single shot gun. Our part of the state required the use of slugs or buckshot, no rifles allowed. I went to the sport shop before season to get the ammunition I needed. Going up to the counter I requested, "One slug please." I can remember the guys behind the counter just looked at me like I had a screw loose. With total seriousness, I told them I had a single shot and could shoot only one deer so therefore needed only one slug.

One other reason, which I did not tell them, was a slug cost nearly twenty cents each, which was rather expensive in my thrifty mind. It would have been interesting to hear them the rest of that day as undoubtedly they had a good laugh at my expense. They did open a box and sold me one slug. The season ended with the slug still unfired. I never gave it a thought to find out how the gun shot slugs and practice with it. Why would I want to shoot twenty cents into a block of wood every time I pulled the trigger? Bottom line is I was not prepared for the hunt that fall, but I did not realize it.

Application: How prepared are we as we rub shoulders with people going to eternity without Christ? How prepared are we for hard times? How prepared are we to walk the Christian life in a world that, in every aspect, is dedicated at satisfying the flesh?

We need ammunition that comes from reading the Scripture and hearing, or reading about sound Bible teachers. Then we need to practice. This is accomplished by living a life in submission to God and by being ready and willing to speak to others of Christ. Just as there was a cost to buy the slug, there will be a cost to be prepared. It will cost time to study. It may cost you a job, people talking about you, or even your life. Whatever the cost, it will be worth the price for the dividends will be paid throughout eternity.

As in today's reading, we are in warfare that we need to be prepared for. The enemy is totally prepared to see that we fail. We need to take our Christianity seriously and realize that the stakes are high for us and those whom we may have the opportunity to witness.

"Put on the whole armour of God, that ye may be able to stand against the wiles of the devil." Ephesians 6:11

Verses: Ephesians 6:10-20

Thinking Out Of The Box

We, as humans, are quite often creatures of habit. Our comfort zone is our box, and we tend to greatly dislike getting out. The animals we hunt are quite the same way. Game trails can be observed all over the country to varying degrees. When hunting in Alaska for caribou, the terrain was covered with small hummocks. They were maybe a foot high and two foot around. This is typical of tundra, so I am told. The walking was extremely difficult unless you got on a caribou trail. Over the many years of herd movement, they wore a groove in the earth's surface. This trail would be smooth and well worn so that it was easier to walk among the hummocks. These animals, as well as others, will use this trail to get from bedding to feeding areas, or to migrate to another area. Most other animals as well as birds have the same tendencies and use ground and air patterns which will give them resting places and a good supply of food. There is security for the animal as it follows where they and others have traveled before. This habit can be the quarry's undoing. They can be patterned and hunted when these routes are discovered. What was the animals' security and comfort can also be its demise.

Application: Christians can bring this type of mentality into church ministry. We want to follow what others have done before. We may have done it the same way for years, and there is safety and security in that. Our little box is well defined, and we know exactly what, when, where, how, and why to respond to every scenario that may arise. The danger in this is that we have ruled out the working of the Holy Spirit. I believe God is very creative with unlimited imagination. Look at creation, and Scripture itself to get a glimpse of this truth. Quite often, God uses different approaches and techniques in dealing with His people in the Old Testament as well as the Church in the New Testament. Our unwillingness to think outside the box and keep following tradition and former ways can lead to the death of the church and stunted growth for the individual. I just recently read a slogan, "If the horse is dead, dismount." In other words if the old way of doing things is not all that successful then try another method. Do not misunderstand, there should be no compromise on the Word of God; but there can be changes made concerning methods in area ministry. What could God accomplish through us if we would be willing to get out of the way and let the Holy Spirit do as He wishes?

"If we live in the Spirit, let us also walk in the Spirit."
Galatians 5:25

Verses: Ephesians 4:30; Colossians 2:8; Galatians 5; Matthew 6:7

A Gentle Patience

Behind our house is a small farm pond. It has been a focal point for the grandchildren during the summer. They spend hours swimming and fishing in it. This grandpa has had the pleasure of teaching them to fish. Putting on the worms, casting, and taking the fish off the hook comes more natural to some than others. There are times when my patience gets strained, such as when the brake does not get released properly or the reel was cranked backwards and the result is a tangled mess. The bass and bluegill seem to have an insatiable appetite for the worms that are fed to them. Needless to say, we go through more worms than actual fish caught. The enjoyment level of the children seems to be directly related to the patience level of myself. When all have tired of fishing, we go to the house, clean the fish, and head directly to the kitchen to fry them up. The fruit of their labor is a delight to their palate.

Application: Have you ever stopped to think of our Heavenly Father and the role He takes as we go through life? He is so patient with us and gently instructs us whether it is in our daily walk or a new area where we are stepping out in faith. We fail, and He just meets us where we are and continues to guide us. We must ask ourselves if we are patient with others. Is there a gentle guidance even though the other person may have made the same mistake before? Am I as patient with others as God is with me? The fruit of our labor will be enjoyed throughout eternity.

"Behold, we count them happy which endure. Ye have heard of the patience of Job, and have seen the end of the Lord; that the Lord is very pitiful, and of tender mercy." James 5:11

Verse: James 5:7-11

Giving And Receiving

Eight years ago a medical situation rendered my balance defunct. Now I need to walk with aid otherwise I tend to stagger and fall. When I move, the objects I am looking at appear to jump and shake. Early on, before the actual diagnosis, Gary and I went turkey hunting. Hiking across a field in the pre-dawn hours, my course veered off from the originally intended direction. Shortly after that, I fell. Gary helped me the rest of the way with us both silently laughing at the sight this all must have presented. A few years later, during duck hunting, we had to walk a trail again in the pre-dawn hours to get to a choice spot in a bay on Lake Michigan. The only way for me to be able to do this was for us to let the others go ahead, and again, Gary helped me out to our spot. This was a bit humiliating in front of the other guys, as a result, I intended not to go the next year. At the insistence of my friend, I relented and because of his help had a great time. This is a beautiful picture of a truth that God desires for us to grasp.

Application: In a spiritual sense I think this is what God is saying in Galatians 6, where we are instructed to help restore a fellow believer. We are to come along side, give them an arm, and provide support. We need to ask ourselves, am I willing to offer help to a brother? Am I willing to receive help from a brother? As we humble ourselves and either give or receive that help, we will find that our walk will be much more enjoyable. Are we willing to yield ourselves and do as God desires and reap the benefits?

"Brethren, if a man be overtaken in a fault, ye which are spiritual, restore such an one in the spirit of meekness; considering thyself, lest thou also be tempted. Bear ye one another's burdens, and so fulfil the law of Christ."
Galatians 6:1, 2

Verse: Galatians 6:1-5; Matthew 18:15-20

Armchair Hunter

Most of my hunting and fishing has been quite localized. I have had the opportunity to take some trips, but my experiences fall short of my dreams. The main reason stopping me from going to exotic places is the same for most; too much month at the end of the money. With this dilemma, I have become an armchair hunter. I enjoy the stories hunters and fishermen have written of far off places. The advantage is there are no marathon flights, no malaria pills to be taken, no deadly encounters with mammals or reptiles, but there is also no satisfaction of a personal adventure. It is still someone else's adventure.

Application: We have to ask ourselves, am I an armchair Christian? Do we have excuses not to become involved in the work of our Lord? God has given each of us the ability to do something for Him. Often times we look at the men and women of God who seem to accomplish much, and we dream of their adventures with God. We may not be endowed to reach the masses or to do the great things others have been asked of God, but are we doing what we can? Is God telling us to get up from the armchair and engage in the battle? Is our goal to finish this life strong for the Lord by doing all He has enabled us to do? Will we do what we can even though it may seem inconsequential? Respond to God. ENGAGE!

"I have fought a good fight, I have finished my course, I have kept the faith:" II Timothy 4:7

Verse: I Corinthians 9:24-27; I Timothy 6:12; II Timothy 4:1-8

The Trophy Feast

As I am writing, I look upon the walls of my living room and see several trophies hanging. These trophies are not record book quality, but are representative specimens of their kind. I am not what one would call a trophy hunter, but am more for the procurement of meat. I know some will say a meat hunter is a trophy hunter "wanna-be," but, for me, I enjoy the meal that comes from the hunt.

We have made it a family practice to have the evening meal together. When I cook the fish or game, I tend to do a lot of experimentation with seasonings and herbs. Most turn out quite edible, but there are some that would fall into the category of a do-not-repeat. Along with the meal, there is usually a lot of conversation covering a variety of topics. As a family, we learn more of each other, our burdens, our dreams, our victories and the experiences of the day.

Application: This makes my mind go to the book of Revelation, to the marriage supper of the Lamb. Give me the liberty to use my imagination here... the event as it unfolds. This feast is in honor of the Groom, who is Jesus Christ, and the bride, who is the Church. The food is beyond compare, the aroma is inconceivable, and the flavors quite exquisite. We sit with God the Father and His Son, Jesus, and host of angels all around the room. The singing and conversations are covering a whole gamut of subjects, but always returning to the focal point of our love, which is Jesus.

Just think how much greater the joy and excitement will be at this heavenly feast in comparison to our earthly experiences. Thank you, Jesus, for providing a way for us to be a partaker in this heavenly feast.

"Let us be glad and rejoice, and give honour to him: for the marriage of the Lamb is come, and his wife hath made herself ready." Revelation 19:7

Verse: Revelation 19:7-10

Sizing Up The Hunt

Some time ago, I went to Alaska with a hunting buddy to hunt caribou while he hunted moose. It was a fantastic time, and we saw sights that were breathtaking. We enlisted the help of an outfitter because of legalities and to help ensure a positive hunt experience. As we sat on what a flatlander would call a mountain, I began to realize this guide was well versed in animal behavior. He knew where to find caribou and where we could observe moose and bear. His job was to put me onto caribou, help size up the animal, read the weather, and so much more. He used his many years of experience to accomplish this. My job was to follow him and listen to his advice, then shoot the caribou without messing up the shot. We had a great time and he succeeded to put me onto a decent caribou on the next to last day. It is now featured as a trophy on my living room wall. The success of the hunt depended largely on his ability to locate game, and my willingness to follow him regardless if I understood his reasoning or not.

Application: Isn't this what we experience in the Christian life? The Holy Spirit is our guide. He knows what we need. He knows the pitfalls and the lay of the land. He will keep us on the proper path and not let us wander off. The kicker is that we are to follow. This is the part that can be difficult, as we want to explore and go our own way. We do not see the dangers or the opportunities. If we want to be "successful" as a Christian, we need to follow the guidance of the Holy Spirit. We are told in Scripture to follow after righteousness and, in doing so, we will please God.

"For this God is our God for ever and ever: he will be our guide even unto death." Psalm 48:14

Verse: Psalm 48:11-14; Matthew 4:18-22; Proverbs 15:9

Oh, Taste And See

At the risk of being too obvious, there are two areas that humans and animals have in common. We both need food and water. Both of our existences require the intake of liquid and nourishment. Death will be the result without it. There are stories of thirsty animals rushing headlong toward water when they smell it even from a distance. We utilize this knowledge when we are looking for a place to hunt and take advantage of either food or water sources to set up our blinds.

Application: We read in the book of Psalms, how God's Word and the time spent alone with Him are essential to the Psalmist. We have to ask ourselves just how important is God's Word to us. Do we consider His Word and our time with Him as a matter of life and death? Our spiritual vitality is at stake. For us to ignore drinking in God's Word and feasting on His presence will cause us to shrivel up in our spiritual life and growth will not take place. To be alive and effective for God, we cannot overlook the need to feed our spiritual self. Are we hungering and thirsting after God?

"My soul thirsteth for God, for the living God: when shall I come and appear before God?" Psalms 42:2

Verse: Psalm 42:1-11; I Peter 2:1-3; Hebrews 5:11-14

Focused And Tuned In

There is a monster buck in a given area. You have patterned him and know his every habit. Before season, you go out and put up the tree stand and trim away a shooting path through the brush. Opening day comes and you are out early despite the fact that he is not seen until five o'clock in the afternoon on your scouting tours. By three thirty, your senses are beginning to tune in for the arrival of the big boy. You listen so intent your ears hurt, and you are getting a headache. A rabbit hops in, and you can hear it munch on grass. A leaf falls from a tree twenty feet away, and it sounds like a tree falling. Time is ticking; it is four thirty. Tired of sitting, you try to ignore the numb feeling in your legs. The anticipation is getting stronger the closer it gets to five o'clock. Then there is a soft and almost unheard crunch of a distant leaf. Your every fiber goes into overdrive. Ears straining, fingers gripping the weapon, hands trembling, as there is another sound of footfall. It is certain that it is not a squirrel but something larger. Your focus is on the sound and its movement in every direction. Not wanting to move, you rotate your eyes until you can see the back of the sockets. Then there is silence. The tension is unbearable. Suddenly, there he is, the biggest buck you have ever seen. He steps into the shooting lane and pauses. You aim, fire, and now, the fine trophy is yours.

Imagine the same scenario except at four thirty you realize that you hear too much road noise. An ambulance goes by with sirens blowing, work just let out and there is increased traffic, and then three walkers pass by talking loudly. You loose concentration and cannot listen as you should. Agitated by the distractions, you lose focus. The soft crunch of leaves is unnoticed, and you fail to be prepared for the big boy's appearance. He walks into the shooting lane and passes right on through. The opportunity is missed, and he is not seen again.

Application: God has a desire to commune with us. As in Elijah's experience though, it is usually in a still small voice He accomplishes this. He will not run competition with other "noises." He wants us focused and tuned in to Him. Too often, we are focused on distractions and fail to hear Him and miss out on opportunities that are given to us. We miss out on offering help or encouragement to our spouse or fellow employee. We miss out on the special teaching and listening opportunities that are given to us with our children. We tend to be focused on careers, sports, hunting, or whatever our individual interests. I wonder of the times I have not heard God and have missed out on a blessing or being a blessing to someone else. We need to take time out for praying, reading His Word, being quiet and seeing what He has for us. When we are in that tree, straining with expectation for the sound of the deer, ask ourselves, "Am I listening with the same eagerness or expectation to what God is trying to say to me." I cannot help but believe God has a great desire to become more intimate with us. What kind of relationship would we have with a loved one if we spoke only a sentence a day to them? That is often what we do to our Heavenly Father in a quick S.O.S. prayer when we are in trouble or a brief meal prayer. We wonder why power has gone out of our Christian life but do not take time to get re-energized by listening to God's still small voice.

"And he said, Go forth, and stand upon the mount before the LORD. And, behold, the LORD passed by, and a great and strong wind rent the mountains, and brake in pieces the rocks before the LORD; but the LORD was not in the wind: and after the wind an earthquake; but the LORD was not in the earthquake: And after the earthquake a fire; but the LORD was not in the fire: and after the fire a still small voice." 1 Kings 19:11, 12

Verse: 1 Kings 19:1-18

Quick Draw

We all realize once the trigger is pulled, whether on a bow or gun, it is too late to change your mind. You have committed the projectile to find a mark, and there is no recalling. Maybe you have experienced the sick feeling of pulling the trigger and knowing instantly it was a poor shot. Maybe you have experienced a snap shot, only to realize that you shot in a direction that could cause damage to person or property. I think we have all been there at one time or another. There is less chance of regret when we take time before pulling the trigger. I remember when I was young; I strapped on a western holster and loaded up my H&R .22 caliber pistol. Feeling the weight of the gun on my hip, I stood and stared down a can on a pile of dirt. Somewhat less graceful than the gunslingers of the western movies, I drew out the gun and fired at the can. The speed was slow and cumbersome, but nevertheless, I had managed to get off a shot. I went to check on the hole that should be in the can; but when I got to it, I discovered the can as well as the dirt was undisturbed. I looked all over the pile to see where I had hit but could not find a trace. I looked beyond the pile to see a hole punched through the steel roof of the barn directly behind the target. Needless to say my quick draw days came to an abrupt end.

Application: An ill word spoken, like a bullet or arrow cannot be recalled. We have been cautioned to think before we speak. This advice is to cause us to be sure of our speech. Problems arise when we let what first comes to mind fly out of our mouth. The hurt that a harsh word can cause, cannot be recalled no matter how badly we feel about it. The book of Proverbs repeatedly states that a wise man will use caution and control of his tongue. The fool will use his tongue in a way that is displeasing to God. We can build up or tear down. We read in James 1, that man can tame the animals and birds, but no man can tame the tongue. This tells us we need to rely upon God to help keep our words gentle. We read in James 3 that we are not to praise God and curse man, and yet so often that is exactly what we do and sometimes think nothing of it. "My brethren, these things ought not so to be." James 3:10

"Wherefore, my beloved brethren, let every man be swift to hear, slow to speak, slow to wrath:" James 1:19

Verse: James 1: 20; James 3:1-12; Proverbs 18:21; Proverbs 21:23

The Great Awaited Day

For many people, November 15th is just another day on the calendar; but for Michigan deer hunters, it is opening day of the gun... deer season. It is a day that has been long anticipated and prepared for. It is easier to get out of bed in the pre-dawn hours on that day than any other day. We get up and turn on the outside light. Even though we may see nothing but dense fog or heavy rain or maybe even a snow blizzard, it does not deter us from the routine re-enacted on an annual basis. Not even being sick is going to slow us down on this day. The day of the week is no problem because we requested the day off far in advance. We can justify the day off when it falls on Sunday in that we can worship God in the great outdoors.

The dawn always comes way too slow and the anticipation for seeing the big buck is the greatest on opening day. At the legal shooting time of 7:00 a.m., there seems to always be shots fired in the distance, and this keeps up for most of the morning. We get a little frustrated hearing this if we are not seeing anything except an occasional chipmunk. But that is hunting and it is why we are driven to get out in the field just in case the big boy comes by.

Some of us, as time passes, have tended to lose the passion for getting out when there are unfavorable weather conditions. We look out the window see the fog, and since nothing can be seen we will roll over and wait for the fog to burn off. The rain or snow should stop, or at least slow down a little, before we venture out. Then the thought of a cold turning into pneumonia is enough to make one pull the covers up a little higher.

Application: The same can be true for the Christian life. We tend to start out with excitement and passion for the ministry. We will stick it out when things get a little trying, and the thought of surrender is not in our vocabulary. Our commitment to Christ and the church is not to be deterred by anything. Then after a time, we may begin to lose the passion, and the trials seem like a wall that cannot be breached. The commitment of going to church and keeping in the ministry begins to wane as outside activities come up. The excitement we once had is getting fainter as other things are becoming more important to us. I wonder... what if Christ had gotten part way to Calvary and His passion for the lost world began to wane, and He laid down the cross and walked away? Sounds ludicrous? Aren't we doing the same when we turn from what is on the heart of Christ, and choose to wimp out? Where is our passion? Where is our excitement? Where is our commitment? If it is lessoning, maybe we need to get a fresh look at Christ, who He is and the burden that is upon His heart. Let us go out of this life working our fingers to the bone for Christ.

"... choose you this day whom ye will serve; whether the gods which your fathers served that were on the other side of the flood, or the gods of the Amorites, in whose land ye dwell: but as for me and my house, we will serve the LORD." Joshua 24:15

Verse: Joshua 24:14-28

Shoot It, Then Eat It

A new saying should be "Don't eat your meat before you shoot it." How many times have you had a shot at a bird or animal that was a "sure thing"? You will see it coming in slow and easy. There are no obstacles in the line of fire. You can visualize the animal on the ground, field dressing it, hauling it out, and eventually eating it. You can almost smell it cooking and tasting it as it is served. Then, one of two things happens. The prey turns and the sure shot is gone or you wait, pull up, squeeze the trigger or release the arrow, and instead of fresh meat, there is nothing but air. It was a clean miss. As the scene is replayed in your mind, it is incomprehensible how a shot like that could be messed up. Staring you in the face is the fact that the animal is long gone, with no sign of a hit. You begin to realize maybe more time should have been spent in making sure of proper placement of the shot or your nerves should have quieted a bit more. Overconfidence can be the cause of a miss like this.

Application: Where do we place our confidence when it comes to spiritual issues? We are more apt to rely upon God for strength and direction when we are in an unfamiliar area of ministry or walk of life. We tend to go on our own power when we are working in a familiar area. When we do this we can miss the mark God has in mind for us to hit. There will be missed opportunities and missed relationships as a result. Ask yourselves, what could be accomplished in my life if I humble myself and rely upon God's power in all situations? Only God can fully answer the question but the results will last an eternity.

"But without faith it is impossible to please him: for he that cometh to God must believe that he is, and that he is a rewarder of them that diligently seek him." Hebrews 11:6

Verse: Philippians 1:6; Hebrews 12:1-3

Experiencing The Whole Package

Butchering and meat processing has been a part of my hunting and fishing experience since childhood. If I shot it or caught it, I was to clean it. I have helped a friend, who is a taxidermist/meat processor, cut and package deer other hunters have tagged. I think a hunter who sends his game out is missing a great education and realization of how awesome God has created living creatures. I constantly marvel at the intricacy of the way God has put together the skeleton and the muscle groups of the body. There are muscle groups that lie beside each other but are independent of each other, having their own purpose. The functions cannot take place without the brain sending signals to the various parts.

Application: The application is twofold. First, we must realize God has created us in a complex fashion. I am amazed one could think we came from pond scum. In Jeremiah, we read God knew Jeremiah before He created him. Matthew tells us every hair on our head is numbered. David tells us in Psalms how completely and intimately God knows our every action, thought, and motive. Today, revel in the fact that the God of the universe knows you. He cares for you and has created you for a purpose. It is humbling and exhilarating. Does our life reflect that we are His creation? Do we function in the knowledge that He is aware of our every thought and action?

Second, we are part of the body of Christ. He is the head from which we are to receive signals. Often we get the idea that we are in control and can do our own thing instead of God being in control. We, as different members of the body tend to think we are independent from each other, however, it is unfeasible to be entirely independent of the rest of the body. When one part of the body is hurting or injured, the whole body is affected and the ministry will not proceed as God had intended. We must ask ourselves, "Am I functioning in the body as Christ has intended?"

"And whether one member suffer, all the members suffer with it; or one member be honoured, all the members rejoice with it." I Corinthians 12:26

Verse: Jeremiah 1:4-5; Matthew 10:24-33; I Corinthians 12:12-31

No Waiting Required

This is the age of instant food, instant purchases, and instant gratification of all sorts. If there is something that is needed or wanted, one can get in the car, go on E-Bay, or on the telephone and get it. There is no waiting required. This can get one into serious trouble financially because there will come a time when the piper has to be paid. With instant gratification mentality, I sometimes go to the woods or get into the boat and find it hard to sit back, be patient, and wait for something to happen. If it is slow, I may change locations or tactics in an effort to get the results I desire. In doing so, there have been times when I have blown a chance to score on game. I get a quick glimpse of it's backside as it escapes or hear the sound of it running off. There are times when moving is justified if there is no fish or game in the area, but often, the move made is premature.

Application: We can bring this philosophy of instant gratification into the spiritual life as well. What is our response when we are waiting upon God for an answer to prayer that seems to be taking too long? His "wait" answer can be excruciating to us as we chomp at the bit and want to get on with it. Patience in the times of trials and tribulations can also be a valued commodity which is hard to obtain. In James, we read that testing and trials can produce patience and make us complete, so why do we want to rush through these times? We want the results that come from these experiences, but we do not want to take the time, effort, and pain to get there. We read in Philippians that God has begun a good work in us that will take a lifetime to complete. Do we have the patience to let Him do as He wills in our life? Thankfully, God has patience with us as we seek in vain instant spirituality. We need to realize it is a lifetime process, and there are no shortcuts.

"Being confident of this very thing, that he which hath begun a good work in you will perform it until the day of Jesus Christ:" Philippians 1:6

Verse: James 1; Philippians 1:1-6

Keep Your Eyes On The Light

I have never been really lost, but there have been two times when I was a bit turned around. I knew generally where I was but not sure how to get out of my situation, you may have an idea of what I mean. The first time this happened was on a fifteen acre woods after dark, following a blood trail of a deer. I knew if I followed a straight line I would come out at the road or field so I was not lost. My point of reference was a yard light at the neighbors. I would follow the trail, circle when I lost it, and every once in a while check on the location of the light through the trees. What I did not realize is that the neighbor to the west also had a yard light. The point of reference had a 180 degree shift and when I thought I was facing east, I may have been facing west. I was getting tired and getting nowhere because of taking my eyes off the point of reference and then following the wrong light. I felt like a pinball. Finally, by keeping my sight on the light, I got out to the east then found out later of the yard light to the west.

The second time was when we tracked my daughter's deer. The group came in from hunting at dark to learn of her hit. We went out into the night and began to follow the blood trail. At first there was no problem, but after a time, the trail entered into the big woods. The terrain was hilly and, at times, quite thick with undergrowth. I had been in this part of the woods often and felt as though I knew exactly where we were. The problem was that the reference points I saw were not what I was picturing in my mind. As we traveled through the woods, we saw a yard light so I calculated where we were; except that the light was not the one I thought it was and I'm still not sure which one it was. Afterward, we came to a wide lane. I knew there was only one spot that would look like that, but I thought I must be wrong because I was convinced we were in another area. Then we came to a clearing. It was the lake, but how could it be because I was sure we were on the other side of the woods. After I faced up to the facts that we were not where I thought we were, there were no other problems.

Application: As a Christian, our point of reference is to believe God and His Word. If we keep Him in our sight, there will be no problem of staying on track. However, if we take our sight off Him and depend on our own sense of direction, we may be in for a long, hard walk. Like the first scenario with the two lights, which light are we following, true or false? Is the point of reference truly God or is it perhaps another person or ourselves? We can also thank God that He is our constant point of reference as we go through the dark valleys of life.

"Looking unto Jesus the author and finisher of our faith; who for the joy that was set before him endured the cross, despising the shame, and is set down at the right hand of the throne of God." Hebrews 12:2

Verse: Hebrews 12:1-3; Psalm 108:1-9

Success Can Have Regrets

As I get older, I am beginning to understand an interesting thought process that I and others have experienced when hunting. This thought process evokes a reflective emotion immediately following the kill. A feeling of regret or sadness comes over the hunter. In my younger days there was usually only great excitement over the fact that the hunt was a success. Now, a different feeling often comes over me. As I look at the animal on the ground, there is a sense of sadness. This feeling goes beyond the thoughts of the work ahead of retrieving, dressing, cutting, and packaging. It considers the fact that just a few minutes ago you were observing a creature in its natural state. You can touch it with your hands, admire its trophy quality, or just sit down and enjoy the beauty of the animal and reflect on the moments before and after the shot. Some call it giving respect to the animal, but for me, it is to admire God's creation up close and personal and thank Him for His creation and letting me have a tangible part of it.

Application: I think most spouses and parents have regrets when they look back over the years. One of the greatest times of reflection occurs when a child gets married and moves out of the house. One sees where he or she blew it and missed the mark as a parent. There is also a time coming when we will stand before God to give an account of our time while on earth. There will be excitement when experiencing what God has prepared for us in the beauty and majesty of Heaven. Most of all, there will be a thrill of being with Jesus Christ who gave Himself for us. However, we will have a moment of seriousness as we stand before God Almighty while the quality of our earthly works is tried by fire. This will reveal opportunities missed, ministries overlooked, and a life lived in the flesh and not in the Spirit. Have any regrets come to mind while reading this? Ask forgiveness from God and proceed living today with eternity in mind. Choose to live this day forward in such a way that there will be only joy in hearing, "well done good and faithful servant." Father, help me this day to live for You and walk in obedience to Your Word.

"Every man's work shall be made manifest: for the day shall declare it, because it shall be revealed by fire; and the fire shall try every man's work of what sort it is. If any man's work abide which he hath built thereupon, he shall receive a reward. If any man's work shall be burned, he shall suffer loss: but he himself shall be saved; yet so as by fire." 1 Corinthians 3:13-15

Verse: I Corinthians 3:10-15; Matthew 25:23

A Sweet Savor

The market is flooded with all kinds of scents for just about every creature that swims or walks. The scents are to cover up human odor or to make the intended quarry turn to mush and find it irresistible not to come drifting in to the source of the smell. There are even scents that you can put on plastic worms to make fish drool. Years ago, I was bear hunting alone in the woods of Michigan's Upper Peninsula. I went with the assumption there was a bear behind every tree and that coming home with a huge bruin was a sure thing. The closest I came to one was to get a good nose full of an unseen bear's natural ambiance.

I had read that a bear could not resist coming to the smell of anise, so I purchased a bottle and took it to the woods with me. Once in the woods, and before going off into the great unknown, I doused my boots with this bottle of anise. Yes, you read it right. My theory was that no matter where I went I always had the scent on me and they would come to me. Thankfully, that did not happen. I thought about this later and realized how foolish this was. Can you imagine sitting under a tree, dozing off, and waking to a bear licking your boots trying to make a meal of the leather still on your feet?

Application: I am reminded in the book of Revelation that the prayers of the saints are a sweet savour to God. I realize these verses are of a different time (dispensation), but I believe the principle is true for today as well. Our prayers to God are a pleasing aroma to Him. He desires to hear from His children. In II Corinthians, we see our labors of faith and service of spreading the Gospel to the lost is a sweet aroma to God. Similar to the sweet smell of anise for the bears, it is something to be desired. Realizing God is pleased by our proper actions and prayers… is our sweet smelling aroma always before God?

"And the smoke of the incense, which came with the prayers of the saints, ascended up before God out of the angel's hand." Revelation 8:4

Verse: II Corinthians 2:14-17; Revelation 5:8; Revelation 8:3

Ready – Aim - Fire

To increase the odds of hitting a moving target we use shot guns which put multiple projectiles into the air or along the ground. If there was only one shot in the cartridge fired at a duck, after the hunt most of us would be stopping by the grocery store to buy chicken for dinner. When we see the bird in flight, there are certain assessments made as we pull up, take aim, and fire. We observe the distance it is from us, the speed it is traveling, and the safety factor of objects nearby. The goal is to have a target, aim at it, and fire with the intension of hitting it. If the target is unclear or non-existent, we only succeed in making a lot of noise and putting shot in the air.

Application: How many of us go through life without a spiritual goal or dream? We have many dreams and goals for our physical life. We set timetables from early life to death. Our careers are planned all the way up to retirement and beyond. When it comes to our spiritual life we often tend to have no target. What does God want to do in and through us? When there is no definite goal in our sights, then we are like the shot gunner wasting shot into the air. We have no idea if the target has been hit because it is unknown. We need to have goals and dreams in our life so that we will have direction in our daily walk. As different opportunities arise or decisions have to be made, we can prioritize them in terms of our goal. Will the activity or decision help us accomplish our goal or keep us in line with the target? If not, then we need to abandon that avenue. Do you have a spiritual goal God has been laying upon your heart? Are you pursuing a vision or dream at your church? If not, we need to take time with God and seek out what He has for us. Do we want to be busy in trivial activities or in pursuit of a deeper God given goal? In Proverbs, we read that without a vision the people perish or are unrestrained. Paul uses a runner and boxer to illustrate the use of goals for the purpose of winning. We need to have goals in our spiritual life. What is your target? The next step is Ready, Aim, Fire!

"Know ye not that they which run in a race run all, but one receiveth the prize? So run, that ye may obtain." I Corinthians 9:24

Verse: Proverbs 29:18; I Corinthians 9:24-27

Altitude Revelation

We had the opportunity to go to Alaska and enjoy the beauty of that state. Upon flying home, there were two thoughts that came to me.

First Lesson

The first thought, is that we are insignificant compared to the overall scheme of things. We sometimes have an inflated view of ourselves. We compare ourselves with others by the quality of our equipment, the amount of success we enjoy, or the size of the trophies we have gotten. When our perspective is changed, say for example from the airplane at 35,000 feet, we look down and see just how minute we really are. People are just a speck on a speck in the universe. Why is it we can get so puffed up? When we read Job and the Psalms we see man is but a worm. No glory, no airs, nothing of value except for the fact we are created by God. He has placed such a value upon us that He sent His son to die for us so we might have eternal life. Our need of a Savior makes us important to Him, not our successes or our position in life. Realizing God loves such worms as us should inspire us to live more devoted lives for Him.

"For God so loved the world, that he gave his only begotten Son, that whosoever believeth in him should not perish, but have everlasting life." John 3:16

Second Lesson

The second thought from 35,000 feet is a result of the view at night. Some remote areas have light spread many miles apart, but in others there may be clusters of light. The people are not seen, but the light is the result of human presence. Consider that a solitary light may be seen from such an extreme distance. It caused me to think of how our spiritual lights should be shining in a dark world. Is it clear and bright or dim and obscure? God wants us to be of such brilliance that we direct others to Him. Do we need to fan the flame or trim the wick to burn brighter? Are we making a difference? Are we aggressively combating the darkness of sin for the sake of the kingdom of God?

"Ye are the light of the world. A city that is set on an hill cannot be hid. Neither do men light a candle, and put it under a bushel, but on a candlestick; and it giveth light unto all that are in the house. Let your light so shine before men, that they may see your good works, and glorify your Father which is in heaven." Matthew 5:14, 16

Verse: Job 25:6; Ps. 22:6; John 3:16-19

Tethered In The Stand

Every year we hear reports of hunters falling out of trees while hunting. Some are not injured, but others have been crippled or killed. One reason for this is that the safety harness is not used. It is only within the last four years that I began to use a harness. I admit it was a foolish practice since there were times I would momentarily fall asleep. I simply did not want to bother with the procedure of hooking up the straps. The possibility of falling and the ramifications for me and my family began to plague my thinking. I realized not only for myself, but also for them, I needed to anchor myself to the solid tree.

Application: God has given us many safety harnesses to use throughout our Christian Life. Utmost is the Bible. He has given us guidelines to follow that we may stay on the straight and narrow. He has given us believers in the Christian community who have written books or personally exhort us to obey and serve Him. His Holy Spirit indwells us to guide us and to convict us of sin. Another God given safety line is a local body of believers. Our fellow brothers and sisters are to challenge, exhort, and encourage us through life's trials. Like the safety harness to the tree, it is a choice whether or not to use it. Why do we at times refuse to use the safety equipment God has provided? Today, make sure you anchor yourself to the Solid Rock.

"Thy word have I hid in mine heart, that I might not sin against thee." Psalm 119:11

Verse: Hebrews 10:19-25; Hebrews 3:12-13

Devoted To The Chase

Hunting seasons vary in length of time. Various ones seem to go on and on, yet others seem to be over before they start. Our spouses may think that some seasons are entirely too long and it is time to be done. Other spouses may think the season is far too short. There are certain seasons that are so enjoyable it is a disappointment for it to be finished for another year. If the animal or bird is shot on opening day, then there is a sadness that it is over. There may even be times we let game go by without a shot because we do not want our hunting season to end. Most hunters are devoted to the chase and cherish the time spent in the field.

Application: Our time on earth is just a short season. I sometimes wonder how we can be so devoted to temporal things in our life, but when it comes to God we can be so indifferent. We do not aggressively pursue God, and we become callous to the things close to His heart. For some, our season may be coming to an end with little to show for our life. It is not too late to devote our lives to serve God more faithfully. Do not let life continue to fly by and later regret what could have been. Run the race, finish the course, and keep the faith. Wouldn't it be great to live Nathan Hale's sentiment, "I regret that I have but one life to give for my GOD?" There should be excitement in going to Heaven after a successful season of devotion to Christ. Like Paul, are we torn between going to Heaven and staying on earth to accomplish more for Him?

"For to me to live is Christ, and to die is gain."
Philippians 1:21

Verse: Proverbs 20:6; Philippians 1:21-26

God's Creation

At first light there is something surreal about the earth waking up. One can get wrapped up in creation all around you when hunting. The creatures begin to scurry around, and the birds seem to sing clearer and louder as the sun begins to warm up the pre-dawn chill. The fall colors beam with beauty as the sun highlights the day. The waters seem to sparkle with greater clarity. Evening has its own beauty and sounds. As the sun dips low it often paints the stormy skies with brilliant colors. The birds return to the trees to roost and seek the perfect position on a limb. The whole landscape is an awesome result of God's handiwork. God did this for you and me to enjoy.

Application: Dear Lord thank you for Your creation for me to enjoy. Thank You for the beauty and detail in which you have invested in every aspect of nature. It is humbling that You would do all this for my enjoyment; that you are mindful of me and you love me. Help me to use it in the way You intended. Help me to stand up to those who would diminish Your involvement in creation and be a witness to Your handiwork. You carved the valleys and pushed up the mountains. You were the source of the many waters. You made the seasons with complexity. You formed the creatures of the air and fields. You and You alone deserve honor and glory. Thank you, Father. Amen.

"...What is man, that thou art mindful of him? or the son of man, that thou visitest him?" Hebrews 2:6

Verse: Psalm 95; Psalm 66:1-4; Psalm 65:5-13

Anticipation

Why do we hunt? This question may conjure up an array of different thoughts. It may be we are after the meat to fill the freezer for the family or a trophy for the wall. It may be we are after the time away from work, to be alone, or with hunting buddies. Whatever the reason, I think we will agree we enjoy it. From time spent outdoors to matching wits against our given quarry, there are many aspects causing us to look forward to opening day of hunting season. Usually, when seasons come, we are prepared with ammo, guns, bow and arrows, camouflage clothing, and all the needed goodies for the hunt. Sometimes I think we are like kids waiting for Christmas morning. There is excitement and anticipation for what lies ahead. Having said that, there have been times when I realized the night before I had not purchased a license. I have also been known not to be able to find a particular article of clothing in the pre-dawn hours before going out. But for the most part, we are ready and anxious to go.

Application: All too often there are Christians who have forgotten the enjoyment and excitement of their walk with Christ. What was meant to be enjoyable has turned into drudgery and our faces and actions reflect what our hearts feel. James says the trials we face are to be encountered with joy because God has meant it for our growth, for our good and for the good of others. Maybe we need to think back and remember the excitement of walking with Christ and rekindle our love for Him. Remember what He has done and will do for us, and continue to grow in love with Jesus.

Some readers may realize that they are not prepared for eternity. God may be speaking to your heart, that you have no personal relationship with Him. Dear friend, if this is the case don't delay in putting your trust in Him and accept the free gift of salvation.

"...behold, now is the accepted time; behold, now is the day of salvation." II Corinthians 6:2

Verse: Revelation 2:4-5; James 1:2-4; Ephesians 2:4-9

Prepare Or Despair

Think back with me to the hunting or fishing trips you have planned. Depending upon the duration of the trip, there is a varying amount of preparation needing to be done. There is gear to be bought or taken out of storage and packed. Time is spent at the range to perfect your shooting skills. New line is placed on reels. If the trip will be strenuous, there is time spent in getting your body ready for the riggers awaiting you. As departure nears, your mind wanders more to mental and physical lists of items needed. Excitement rises in direct proportion with time left. Arrangements are made for the responsibilities left behind. If an outfitter is used, there will be last minute e-mails sent, and all fees to be paid. Tickets are purchased from the airlines, and all permits have been filled out and are in your possession. The day of departure arrives and there is a confidence that all is ready, but there is a faint nagging in the back of your mind that something may have been overlooked. There comes a point when these thoughts are shrugged off, and the next leg of the adventure begins.

Application: We can get so wrapped up in preparing for a trip that it can be all consuming. I wonder how well we are prepared for the greatest adventure to come, which is the departure from this life into eternity. The first question looked at is whether we personally booked a flight. Have we embraced Jesus Christ as our Savior? We come into this world with a ticket to hell because of our sinful nature. Jesus has pre-paid a ticket for us to heaven, but we have to accept it. Jesus took the punishment that we deserve for our sins. He died, rose again, and ascended to Heaven. We need to know that if we claim Christ as our Savior, then, all payments and arrangements have been made for our heavenly journey, and there is nothing that we need to do. Do we believe? If so, have we been preparing for departure? What have we done for Christ while going through this life? Sad to say, we are often more concerned with our temporal plans and little time and effort is expended on living for Jesus Christ.

"For by grace are ye saved through faith; and that not of yourselves: it is the gift of God: Not of works, lest any man should boast." Ephesians 2:8, 9

Verse: 1 Corinthians 9:24-27; Matthew 6:19-21; Romans 10:8-10

If you would like to commit your life to Jesus right now, just speak this prayer from your heart to the Lord. -- Dear Jesus, I recognize I am a sinner and only by your grace can I be saved. By faith I accept your gift of salvation. I realize I cannot work or pay my way into heaven. It is only by believing in Christ's death, burial, and resurrection that I will be saved.

Thank you for preparing a way for me to enter eternity. I repent and ask you to forgive me of my sins, I believe you died on the cross and arose again on the third day that I also might live. Thank you for saving me and writing my name in the Lamb's Book of Life. Amen

Contact Author

You may contact the author by the following methods:

Steven Jacobs
13551 Hoffman Rd
Three Rivers, MI 49093
or
htpp://stevenjacobs.wordpress.com

To Order More Copies of This Book

jacobssw@msn.com

269-273-8247